It's as old as time, yet a new and special experience for each person. Love tugs on heart strings and ties two lives into one with a special knot. Sweet moments, tender glances, precious letters, and endearing declarations evidence a uniting of mind and heart, a precious moment when love tunes lives into perfect harmony.

Discover anew the anticipation, the thrill of your very own special love. Recall the first moment you saw him, how she smiled, the tender gaze you shared together when everything fell into place, when your heart was tied to another.

Two souls with
but a single thought,
Two hearts that beat as one.

MARIA LOVELL

You Are the Only One

All my soul

follows you,

love-encircles you—

and I live in being yours.

ROBERT BROWNING

But if you wish me to love you,

could you but see how much

I do love you, you would

be proud and content.

All my heart is yours, sir:

it belongs to you…

CHARLOTTE BRONTË
JANE EYRE

Thou art my life, my love, my heart,
The very eyes of me,
And hast command of every part
To live and die for thee.

ROBERT HERRICK

When you long with all your heart
for someone to love you,
a madness grows there that shakes all sense
from the trees and the water and the earth.

DENTON WELCH

Forget Me Not

If I know

what love is,

it is because

of you.

HERMAN HESSE

Haply I think on thee, and then my state
(Like to the lark at break of day arising
From sullen earth) sings hymns at heaven's gate,
For thy sweet love remembered such wealth brings,
That then I scorn to change my state with kings.

WILLIAM SHAKESPEARE

My very dear Sarah,

The indications are very strong that we shall move in a few days—perhaps tomorrow. Lest I should not be able to write again, I feel impelled to write a few lines that may fall under your eye when I shall be no more…

I have, I know, but few and small claims upon Divine Providence, but something whispers to me…that I shall return to my loved ones unharmed. If I do not, my dear Sarah, never forget how much I love you, and when my last breath escapes me on the battlefield, it will whisper your name…

But, O Sarah! if the dead can come back to this earth and flit unseen around those they loved, I shall always be near you; in the gladdest days and in the darkest nights…*always, always,* and if there be a soft breeze upon your cheek, it shall be my breath, as the cool air fans your throbbing temple, it shall be my spirit passing by…

CONFEDERATE SOLDIER MAJOR SULLIVAN BALLOU
WROTE THIS LETTER TO HIS BELOVED WIFE ON JULY 14, 1861,
SEVEN DAYS BEFORE HE WAS KILLED IN BATTLE.

Give all
to love,
obey thy
heart.

RALPH WALDO EMERSON

You can't reason with your heart;

it has its own laws,

and thumps about things

which the intellect scorns.

MARK TWAIN

Elizabeth's

spirits soon rising to playfulness again,

she wanted Mr. Darcy to account for his having

ever fallen in love with her. "How could you begin?" said she.

"I can comprehend your going on charmingly, when you had once

made a beginning; but what could set you off in the first place?"

"I cannot fix on the hour, or the spot, or the look,

or the words, which laid the foundation.

It is too long ago. I was in the

middle before I knew that

I had begun."

JANE AUSTEN
PRIDE AND PREJUDICE

Wistful Glances

There can be no true love,

even on your own side,

without devotion;

devotion is the exercise of love,

by which it grows.

ROBERT LOUIS STEVENSON

Mirror your sweet eyes in mine, love,

See how they glitter and shine!

Quick fly such moments divine, love,

Link your lithe fingers in mine!

Lay your soft cheek against mine, love,

Pillow your head on my breast;

While your brown locks I entwine, love,

Pout your red lips when they're prest!

Mirror your fate, then, in mine, love;

Sorrow and sighing resign:

Life is too short to repine, love,

Link your fair future in mine!

J. ASHBY STERRY

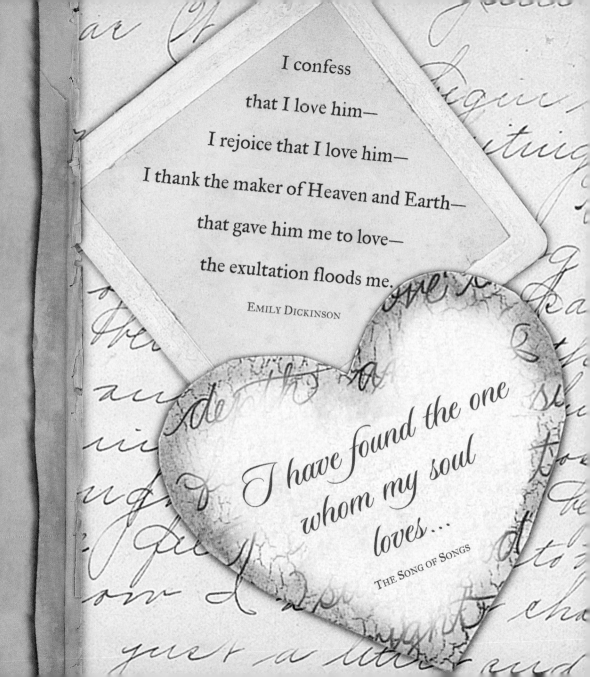

I confess

that I love him—

I rejoice that I love him—

I thank the maker of Heaven and Earth—

that gave him me to love—

the exultation floods me.

EMILY DICKINSON

I have found the one whom my soul loves...

THE SONG OF SONGS

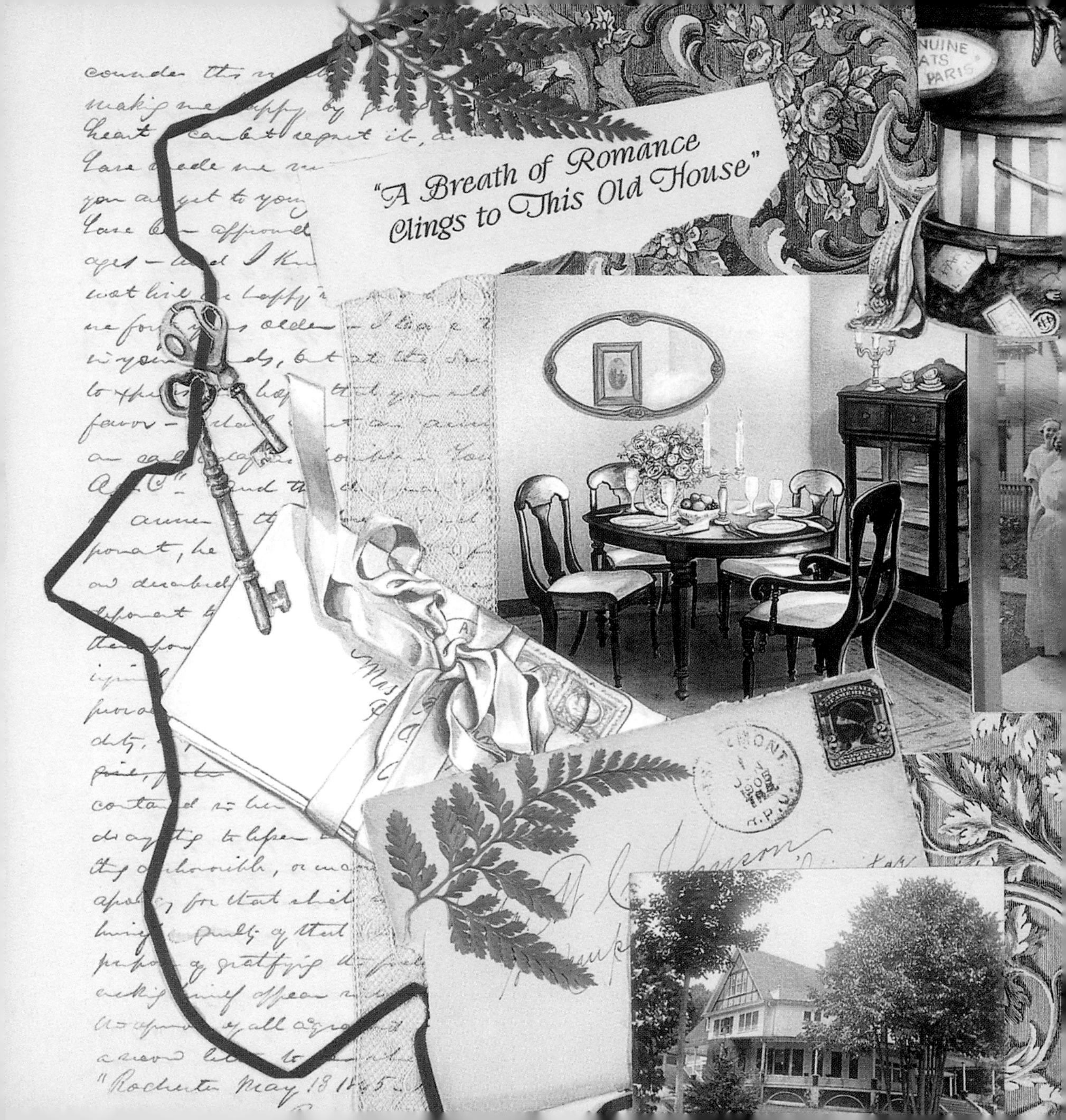
"A Breath of Romance Clings to This Old House"

You have lifted my very soul

up into the light of your soul,

and I am not ever

likely to mistake it

for the common daylight.

ELIZABETH BARRETT BROWNING

"You are part of my existence, part of myself.

You have been in every line I have ever read, since

I first came here, the rough common boy whose poor heart

you wounded even then. You have been in every prospect

I have ever seen since—on the river, on the sails of the ships,

on the marshes, in the clouds, in the light, in the darkness,

in the wind, in the woods, in the sea, in the streets.

You have been the embodiment of every graceful fancy

that my mind has ever become acquainted with.

The stones of which the strongest London buildings

are made are not more real, or more impossible

to be displaced by your hands, than your presence

and influence have been to me, there and everywhere,

and will but remain part of my character,

part of the little good in me..."

CHARLES DICKENS
GREAT EXPECTATIONS

At the touch of love,
everyone becomes a poet.

PLATO

There is a song sung in my heart,
That no one else had heard,
But when my soul was faced with yours,
Your heart knew every word,
The melody was sweet as honey,
The words were lovely and true,
It couldn't be bought
    with treasure or money,
It waited just for you.

GAY TALBOTT BOASSY

Beauty

All beautiful you are,
my darling;

there is no flaw
in you.

THE SONG OF SONGS

Beauty 1915

"Memories and golden days,

Past recall,
beyond our gaze;
Wishes for sweet days to be.
This is what
I send to thee."

"When your twilight dreams are
weaving
Fancies
free,
May thy
fond
affection cleaving
Twine round me, . . .
Thus my wish
of wishes
True shall be."

My Friend

POST CARD

such a
crowned the
tion and with tear
of fire."—"Yo
I can not love him
to be noble a
All voices p
can
...la, "I would
call upon your
...ivia, and sing
...nd among
O you
...but you
" said Olivia: "what
...ove my fortunes, yet
...ivia now reluctantly
...er, and tell him,
...unless perchance
...e aga...to te
Olivia repeated the ...fortunes, yet my state
I am a gentleman. And s...aloud, "I will be
...he is; his tongue, his face, his li...s, action, and spirit,
...y show he is a gentleman." And then she wished

Then Davy and I found ourselves alone in front of the fire. Her eyes, I had not failed to observe, were indeed beautiful: long eyes, grey eyes with a hint of sea-green in certain lights. A wide brow and a small determined chin—a heart-shaped face.

SHELDON VANAUKEN
A SEVERE MERCY

She walks in beauty, like the night

Of cloudless climes and starry skies;

And all that's best

of dark and bright

Meet in her aspect and her eyes:

Thus mellow'd to that tender light

Which heaven to gaudy day denies.

LORD BYRON
"SHE WALKS IN BEAUTY"

Her fresh and innocent eyes

Had such

a star of

morning in

their blue,

That all neglected places of the field,

Broke into nature's music

when they saw her.

TENNYSON
"AYLMER'S FIELD"

gave him the disgraceful appellation
wished to avoid a quarrel with Tybalt
he was the kinsman of Juliet, and mu
the name of a Capulet, which was
rather a charm to allay resent
excite fury. So he tried to
saluted mildly by the name of
Montague, had some secret
but Tybalt would hear
Mercutio, who knew
peace with Tybalt
as a sort of ca
to the pros
and Me

The Sensational Ballad Song
HERE AM I—
Broken Hearted

A   D   F#

There she is—

My old g'al

There

my old pal, and here am

Brok-en   heart

ROMEO AND JULIET

Love is like a violin.

The music may stop

now and then,

but the strings

remain forever.

Anonymous

Art thou gone so, love?
    Lord, my husband, friend,
I must hear from thee every day i' th' hour,
For in a minute there are many days—
by this count I shall be much in years
Ere I again behold my Romeo.

Romeo, Romeo,
        wherefore art thou Romeo?
Deny thy father and refuse thy name;
Or if thou wilt not, be but sworn my love
And I'll no longer be a Capulet.

WILLIAM SHAKESPEARE
ROMEO AND JULIET

In the arithmetic of love,
one plus one equals everything,
and two minus one equals nothing.

"It is a long way to Ireland...Are you anything akin to me, do you think, Jane?"

I could risk no sort of answer by this time: my heart was full.

"Because," he said, "I sometimes have a queer feeling with regard to you—especially when you are near me, as now: it is as if I had a string somewhere under my left ribs, tightly and inextricably knotted to a similar string situated in the corresponding quarter of your little frame. And if that boisterous channel, and two hundred miles or so of land come broad between us, I am afraid that cord of communion will be snapt; and then I've a nervous notion I should take to bleeding inwardly."

CHARLOTTE BRONTË
JANE EYRE

Someday When Dreams Come True

Let love

be your

greatest aim.

THE BOOK OF I CORINTHIANS

Someday when dreams
Come True

2306. Decorating for the Wedding.

Her image accompanied me even in places the most hostile to romance. On Saturday evenings when my aunt went marketing I had to go to carry some of the parcels. We walked through the flaring streets...noises converged in a single sensation of life for me: I imagined that I bore my chalice safely through a throng of foes. Her name sprang to my lips at moments in strange prayers and praises which I myself did not understand. My eyes were often full of tears (I could not tell why) and at times a flood from my heart seemed to pour itself out into my bosom. I thought little of the future. I did not know whether I would ever speak to her or not or, if I spoke to her, how I could tell her of my confused adoration. But my body was like a harp and her words and gestures were like fingers running upon the wires.

JAMES JOYCE
"ARABY," DUBLINERS

I would live in your love

as the sea-grasses live in the sea,

Borne up by each wave as it passes,

drawn down by each wave that recedes;

I would empty my soul of the dreams

that have gathered in me,

I would beat with your heart as it beats,

I would follow your soul as it leads.

SARA TEASDALE

You soothe my soul,

you fill it with so

tender a sentiment

that it is sweet to live...

JULIE DE L'ESPINASSE

Love Me

Brown-thrush singing all day long
In the leaves above me,
Take my love this April song,
"Love me, love me, love me!"

When he harkens what you say,
Bid him, lest he miss me,
Leave his work or leave his play,
And kiss me, kiss me, kiss me!

SARA TEASDALE

e, for
I no
pas-
being
ame,
name
At
king

son
dis-
t, of
rds,
orm,
dis-
iffer-

Daisey's Dimples

Little dimples so sweet and soft,
Love the cheek of my love:
The mark of Cupid's dainty hand,
Before he wore a glove.

Laughing dimples of tender love
Smile on my darling's cheek;
Sweet hallowed spots where kisses lurk,
And play at hide and seek.

Fain would I hide my kisses there
At morning's rosy light,
To come and seek them back again
In silver hush of night.

J. ASHBY STERRY

His heart beat faster and faster as Daisy's white face came up to his own. He knew that when he kissed this girl, and forever wed his unutterable visions to her perishable breath, his mind would never romp again...So he waited, listening for a moment longer to the tuning-fork that had been struck upon a star. Then he kissed her. At his lips' touch she blossomed for him like a flower and the incarnation was complete.

F. SCOTT FITZGERALD, *THE GREAT GATSBY*

When Time Stands Still

So Jacob served seven years to get Rachel, but they seemed like only a few days to him because of his love for her.

THE BOOK OF GENESIS

Because You Love Me

Because you love me, I have found

New joys that were not mine before;

New stars have lightened up my sky

With glories growing more and more.

Because you love me I can rise

To the heights of fame and realms of power;

Because you love me I may learn

The highest use of every hour.

Because you love me I can choose

To look through your dear eyes and see

Beyond the beauty of the Now

Far onward to Eternity.

Because you love me I can wait

With perfect patience well possessed.

Because you love me all my life

Is circled with unquestioned rest.

Yes, even Life and even Death

Is all unquestioned and all blest.

OLD *PALL MALL* MAGAZINE ARTICLE

Love that lasts

I Love You Truly

Where true Love burns

Desire is Love's pure flame.

It is the reflex of our earthly frame,

That takes its meaning

from the nobler part,

And but translates

the language of the heart.

SAMUEL TAYLOR COLERIDGE

In our orchard I saw you picking dewy apples

with your mother (I was showing you the way).

I had just turned twelve years old, I could reach

the brittle branches even from the ground:

how I saw you! how I fell in love!

how an awful madness swept me away!

VIRGIL

What greater thing

is there for two human souls than

to feel that they are joined together

to strengthen each other in all labour,

to minister to each other in all sorrow,

to share with each other in all gladness,

to be one with each other in

the silent unspoken

memories?

GEORGE ELIOT

Ribbons, Roses & Lace

Just as there
comes a warm sunbeam
into every cottage window,
so comes love—
born of God's care
for every separate need.

NATHANIEL HAWTHORNE

How do I love thee? Let me count the ways.
I love thee to the depth
    and breadth and height
My soul can reach,
    when feeling out of sight
For the ends of Being and ideal Grace.

ELIZABETH BARRETT BROWNING
SONNETS FROM THE PORTUGUESE

TELL ME, DEAREST, WHAT IS LOVE

Tell me, dearest, what is love?
'Tis a lightning from above,
'Tis an arrow, 'tis a fire,
'Tis a toy they call desire;
'Tis a smile that doth beguile
The poor hearts of men that prove.

NEW SONGS A-LA-MODE
A RESTORATION SONG BOOK OF 1670

Among my favorite memories,
Are times we spend together,
The sweetness of those
pleasant times,
I keep with me forever,
I take them out and remember,
When you are out of sight,
Our laughing voices fill the air,
And fade into the night.

GAY TALBOTT BOASSY

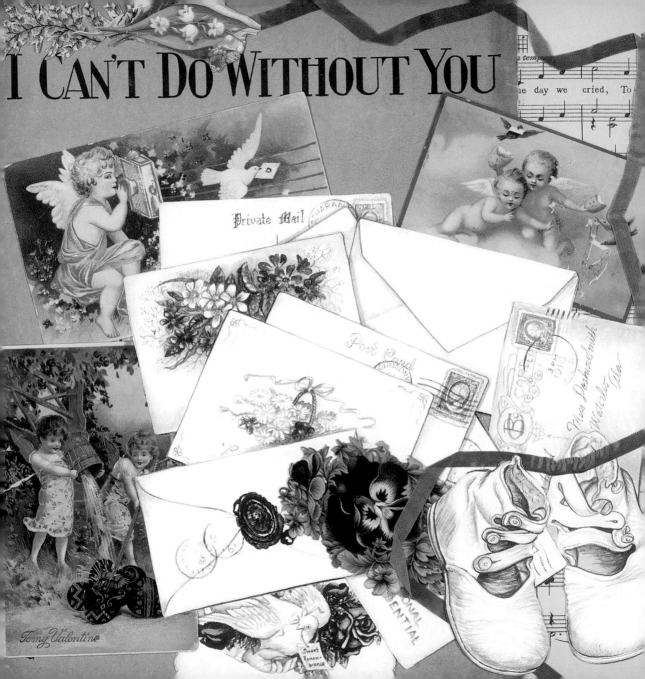

I Can't Do Without You

We are
each of us angels
with only one wing,
and we can only fly
embracing each other.

LICIANO DE CRESCENZO

My eyes skimmed over the words, just barely taking in the sense, hunting for other words. Then I found them and it was like coming to a water hole on the prairie.

"I have thought of you steadily since you left. Without you this place is as empty as the stadium. I had to go to the library to return the books I had out and I looked in our room over at your table by the window. I resented seeing someone else there...."

MILDRED WALKER, WINTER WHEAT

After a moment the sense of waste and ruin overcame him. There they were, close together and safe and shut in; yet so chained to their separate destinies that they might as well have been half the world apart.

"What's the use—when will you go back?" he broke out, a great hopeless How on earth can I keep you? crying out to her beneath his words.

EDITH WHARTON, THE AGE OF INNOCENCE

Love, like a lamp,
needs to be fed
out of the oil of another's heart,
or its flame burns low.

HENRY BEECHER

He Loves Me

You have

stolen my heart

with one glance

of your eyes...

THE SONG OF SONGS

"He Loves Me"

For love is a flower that grows in any soil,
works its sweet miracles undaunted by
autumn frost or winter snow, blooming
fair and fragrant all the year, and blessing
those who give and those who receive.

LOUISA MAY ALCOTT
LITTLE MEN

I'll love you, dear, I'll love you
Till China and Africa meet
And the river jumps over the mountain
And salmon sing in the street.

I'll love you till the ocean
Is folded and hung up to dry
And the seven stars go squawking
Like geese about the sky.

W. H. AUDEN

Faith
goes up the stairs
that love has made and looks
out of the windows which hope has opened.

CHARLES SPURGEON

Faintly her young heart trembles, and the fringe

Lifts from the dewy wells of her eyes;

Her thin cheek deepens to a pale rose tinge—

And doth she love him? Hush! that look replies.

ALICE CARY

Keepsakes from
the One I Love

To love
is to receive
a glimpse
of heaven.

KAREN SUNDE

True Love

True love is
the only heart disease
that is best left to "run on" —
the only affection of the heart
for which there is no help,
and none desired.

MARK TWAIN

Together

How happy am I, having you at my side,

Through life's ever changeable weather;

My hopes and my fears unto you I confide,

As we move heart in heart on together.

We have tasted success, we have drank of desire,

With hearts light and gay as a feather;

And the day and the deeds that our spirits inspire—

We have lived and enjoyed them together.

Through care and misfortune and trouble and pain

Made part of life's changeable weather,

And sickness and sorrow came once and again,

We met and endured them together.

So together still sharing what fate has in store,

May we go to the end of our tether;

When the good and the evil things all are shared o'er,

May we share the last sleep still together.

HUNTER MACCULLOUGH